VENuS
LOOKING AT THE MOON

Colin Macanulty

PublishAmerica
Baltimore

FOR DAVICA WITH
BEST REGARDS

Colin Macanulty

First printing

PublishAmerica has allowed this work to remain exactly as the author
intended, verbatim, without editorial input.

ISBN: 978-1-4489-7254-8 (softcover)
ISBN: 978-1-4489-6390-4 (hardcover)
PUBLISHED BY PUBLISHAMERICA, LLLP
www.publishamerica.com
Baltimore

Printed in the United States of America

THE PROLOGUE........."

We bring you to witness
a clasp of time, when
into the violent world
came love and music.
A love never before seen
on the western earth;
of words and gestures.
Of good fortune, with
music tempering
and softening
wild hearts.
Engendering dreams
with endless passion
blessed, from all quarters,
above all conditions
of human mind and heart,
no matter the many ways
conceived to heaven.
It shows, if you but attend,
there will always be.....
Someone to love.

Kerrisdale

A LOVER'S COMPLAINT

'Goodsir! I heard you were a poet.
A poet with so few words!'
Do your feelings hear only
the screech of the owl?
Are there such feelings
left by for the midsummer day?
What dreams doth the darkness
bring from a midnight bird
that we know cannot sing?
Does the brevity of winter light
deny lovers command of the day?
Just as the sun awakes us all
from our dangling dreams
what then of the morning cries
when the sky plucks its dew
and the pale moon rests its eyes.
Which, if we could but recall,
and so hustle all from heaven
at our request, would our fate
stand still if we had the will.

Kerrisdale

THE SPRING DID COME UPON US

What right have I
to climb the vine
or be lit by the fire
in your lovely eye?
Every time you say..
Anon! Anon! I desire
all thy doubts be gone.
The actors have polished
the boards, every scene
and scent is new, and now
only the cheeks of the rose
will do.
If thy breast be my pillow
I shall not breathe or sleep
and every promise I promise
not to disturb but to keep.
If I could love you
would I not run riot
with absence of thought
from worldly bromides?
If I could love you
would then I have caught
recounted all the days
and nights I have not.
Of all the dreams
we fail or forget to tell,
will be as if what we leave
undone will make us well.

If on concrete my blossoms fall,
nature still will leap the wall.
The Spring did come upon us
and whatever Nature grows
grew within us all at once.
Though its flowers
cannot feed the flesh
they do affect the blood
bringing it to a head
cosseting the heart
venturing the voice; thus,
the Spring did come upon us.
Veiled in the face, yet
passed down with grace
things will run their course
no matter what the grief
or the failure of remorse.
Nothing is ever complete,
no present or future relief.
So, welcome! Take your seat,
lend me a hand to kiss,
bring wine to the tongue
some flowers to rest among.
I must leave all to your choice
no matter that I should miss,
regret only, the loss of your voice.
What were streams below
and wilderness birds
above doing making music
inside my head? What else
should they do instead?
Then, a shell on the beach

forbade me to fail to listen
and all might still be well.
A winter's tale you made of bliss
and of each story in time that I,
whose gifts had paraded your glory,
ended not finding a hand to kiss
neither in your room nor in the hall
just before we said goodbye.
What we thought was Spring
was a much darker offering.

Kerrisdale

THE SECOND CLEARANCE: A SEA CHANGE

Seabirds whirled with wonder
over how empty the boats were.
The women looked down in vain
from the pier for fish.
Off came their striped aprons
to be quietly stowed away.
They could not bear the death
of the sea that first day;
its life was in their blood.
First came the sheep, now this.

Kerrisdale

THE BEAUTIFUL WOMAN

I came to a strange country
and was told the story
of a temple in the hills
among the cherry trees
where the air was crystal.
And the people said
the monks had a tale
of a beautiful woman who
bathed in a hidden lake
before the early mist rose
and took her to Heaven.
I was brought there by flowers
and floating plum blossoms
the breeze brought down, then
high on the hill I found the lake,
hushed, like the color of jade,
and imagined the woman had gone.
A holy man came forth to show me
where she had entered the water
and said he had spent his life
waiting for her to return.

Kerrisdale

WOMAN WITH A SOFT HEART

Woman with a soft heart
if the first frost doth fall;
then bring above the wines
from cool cellars; perhaps
they will help us recall
those hibernating passions
of desire, seasoning the times
we may have thought were lost.
And many hours like this
will surely safely farther fly
before we must say goodbye.
Nobody knows my dreams
the way you do;
or could touch my hand
the way you do.
Dreams...they rise and fall;
you I can always recall;
as if you had just turned
your head my way yesterday,
the way you do.

Kerrisdale

LET ME DREAM

Shutter up the sun,
close my eyes and
let me dream.
What now but care
disturbs this silence,
desperate for love
as a gipsy for air.
I have waited
until the first flower
was ready to drop;
for gentle swellings
and leavened gossamer;
become as shy as the wren
with the golden crown;
shuttered from the sun
with my eyes closed
this care still a noun.
I will make a wish
and call it a dream.
The gift was given to say
to speak out my poems;
but the wind waited its time
to blow everything away
that should be sublime.
What has there been
that we could not find?
Of all the hands we touch
before day breaks the spell

in all the spaces between
where all should be well
I will make a wish,
and call it a dream.

Kerrisdale

LOVE IS A LADYBIRD

Love is a ladybird,
not afraid to stay
or to do any harm;
love is a ladybird.
Lucky, if yours for a day.
Full of safety and charm.
Love is a ladybird.

Skagen 2005

ALL GREAT LOVE IS MOSTLY SILENT

Strange.........
who would have known
that there was love
in every stone, placed
one above the other
on that little green hill.
Strange.........
that the heart will not fill
the lonely cairn with a lament,
for not every song can show
the love that lovers know
or what their love has meant.
Strange.........
the end of the human condition,
sometimes with a final portent,
rhymes a requiem in a sad song.
Yet set apart, and above the throng,
all great love is mostly silent.

Kerrisdale

OUT OF ALL OUR GHOSTLY SHADOWS

Out of all our ghostly shadows
why do some of the memories stay
when all the others go away?
Out of all our ghostly shadows
could one find a way to know
how to start the picture show?
How can we trace into place
all our bits and portions
all the tracks and motions?
Of all the forms from the haze
out of all our ghostly shadows,
where are the ones
we fail to raise?

Kerrisdale

AN UNKNOWN PLACE

Unknown places
should be lit
by candles
to make them soft
when we find them.
New found lips
should just fit
gently, over those
full of the desire
to kiss them.
Outstretched hands
may touch the kindled
yet trembling face,
leading the other
to love and grace.
Then winter sets in
and logs are split,
yet despite the fire
you lack desire.
If that's the case
with candles unlit
you've found darkness
in an unknown place.

Kerrisdale

FOR ANOTHER DAY

Let me waken vivid Venus
on those lonely mornings
after my love is taken;
then randomly tossed
across wailing wild winds.

Thus, all the random kisses
that weave their winsome way
through each sleepless night
disappear at the speed of light.

Yet, let me then forgive
whoever stole love away
and would not let it live
or miss me for another day.

Kerrisdale

APPLES THAT ALWAYS STAY GREEN

Your gestures your early ways
of touching that string of pearls;
and if you count them
they may tell you the story
of how many short days
just passed between us.
There was many a lonely pier
many a secret wonderful dream
that the rain now washes over.
Why didn't you appear
between Groats and Dover
and love me my dear?
Oh, what could have been!
Now, we are just like apples
that always stay green.

Kerrisdale

HURRY THROUGH AMBER BEFORE IT TURNS RED

And so her hand
would hold me, then
I would understand
that I'd better stop.
If it was the time to go
she'd let loose her hair
and rise up from the chair.
Where is the green?
There…in the bed.
Hurry through amber
before it turns red.
Oh, all the breath
that winds my song
came from her wealth
and now she has gone.

Kerrisdale

A CASCADE OF CREAM

Each night I see your profile in a dream;
but now your mirror looks back at me
your hair flowing down your shoulder
in a cascade of cream, whilst your virtue
still is white.
Perhaps this stolen summer season
left me searching for a talisman
I was sure could not be found;
nerves stretched, overstrung, bound.
Then all the silk fell at my feet;
our liquid lips could meet and linger.
Nor can this ink that stains my finger
forget to show the passions we shall climb
amidst all the clashing passages of time.

Kerrisdale

NOBODY'S PERFECT

For all the world like happenstance
I've found a girl who wants to dance.
Who likes cinnamon on her apple sauce
and shares her lipstick when we pause.
She's a country whose flag unfurled
as she took my hand to share her world.
When each curve of her came into view
I became her patriot, tested and true.
I'd found a girl who is full of romance
even though she knows I cannot dance.
In every contract there should be a clause;
'Nobody's perfect, we all have flaws.'

Kerrisdale

SOLITARY ROSES

You know that all those solitary roses
you left for her in the hole in the wall
sent your lover's face beyond recall.
All those hidden texts in every bloom
meant love could never look at the moon.
Parted crystals just coagulate again
over a heart traced on a frosted pane.
When all the voices all the echoes fly,
life and love may breathe a delicate sigh.
Another lover may yet bring good health,
but that's as far as you'll allow yourself
to forget why you left those solitary roses.

Kerrisdale

FROM THE THISTLES

There was no orchestra behind me.
I seemed to be singing on my own.
I couldn't calculate, could not have known
that at last all my struggles were over
when you came into my garden,
took me from the thistles
and said I was elegant and sweet;
just like the apple tinted roses
you might still place at my feet.

Kerrisdale

COME AWAY SWEET LOVE WITH WINE

Are those soft lips both mine?
I anxiously wait for a sign
with a rose a lily and an iris;
full of hope I may have your kiss.
Will you bring me water or wine?
'I love you' I once heard you say,
now I dread the frost in May.
So come to me on a summer's day;
come away sweet love with wine;
please tell me what I must know
and that we may have far to go.
Bring me heat
when snow
is falling.

Kerrisdale

LOVE TOOK OFF HER BONNET

What heedless calls
upon the heart
does beauty bring?
Each beat that falls,
the step the start
the wanton fling
holds us hostage
through the rage.
Not even fourteen lines
of a Shakespearean sonnet
do justice to the times
love took off her bonnet.

Kerrisdale

WHEN A GENTLE LASS APPEARS

When a gentle lass appears
and is added to the list
of those you haven't kissed;
then the misted eye clears
and the aria she softly sings
with her notes of love begins.
Love is working out your fate
and is searching for a mate.
But if love becomes a stranger
and seems to pass you by,
then please stop and ask: 'why
can't I make another try?'
Whatever keeps is kept.
Whoever cries has wept.

Kerrisdale

SPRING IS HERE TO STAY

I scratched your name
on the window pane;
blew out the candles;
there was light enough.
Then I heard you sing.
If all the music you bring
smites a shivering chord
I'll sweep dead leaves away,
hope, Spring is here to stay.

Kerrisdale

ISOLD

I wish I could say hello
or dare to let you know
what seeing you has done.
Oh why do you sway and walk
and talk the way you do?
The click of your Louis heels
across each tiled floor
beaches me upon your shore.
While trying to rescue the fire
my travail deepens the desire.
Should your sail not be white
it will be so cold
if I cannot hold:
my Isold!

Kerrisdale

AND DAFFODILS FILL CUPS WITH TEARS

Among the flowers of the field
how can we ever try to sleep
without love? As kept to keep
makes absence easier to bear
when no stars salute with wine
and daffodils fill cups with tears
while we add wrinkles to the years.
Then do memories remember, care
for all the ruptures never healed.
Of all the roads love may take
to the ways a heart can break,
then, we must sigh for every sign
that may appear upon the moon,
for they disappear so soon.

Kerrisdale

IT DID NOT GRIEVE US THEN

Perhaps they watch us
from the phantom trees
those winged ghosts, who,
while still able to seize
with wild swoop and cry
could not know they too
were on their way to die?
It did not grieve us then
even though young and true
we did not miss their voice.
It did not grieve us then
we did not feel the loss.
But it may come to us too:
that we may not live again.

Kerrisdale

WOMAN WANDERING ALONE COME HOME

Woman wandering alone come home;
guitars are playing here for you.
See all the names on your wall
hear the voices singing your cue.
Planes and trains are at your call;
woman wandering alone come home.
Alas, I seem to have lost my heart,
and since you do not love me
there is nothing to take your place
but art, and this sad poem.
Woman wandering alone, come home.

Kerrisdale

ANY TERM IS FULL FOR THE GOOD

Wherever the truth is tried
and yet seems to fail,
then should all honest men
still speak out, have it prevail
wherever it is most denied.
Then 'tis not just a passing
passion to protect the weak
that moves the world,
but love that does entail
the deeds of honest men
as proof of truth applied.
For who can tell of a man
who has lived so well than
he who does not fear his maker?
Any term is full for the good
who gather up such credit and
would neither spare nor judge
another's choice of falsehood;
but let their light surely sunder
whichever shadow they are under.

Kerrisdale

FOR US THAT GIFT IS SINGULAR

As you see them tumble out
in each small or large amount,
dreams are not merely meant
for counting your life content
by solstices, risings of the sun,
advances or declines of the moon
but in the strength of love.
In the other intervals
when there is no love
then one must dream alone
of all we once have known.
For us that gift is singular,
but will surely cost the time
it took to write this rhyme.

Kerrisdale

A PROSE POEM...TO SHAKE OUT THE LIFE WE LOSE IN DREAMS

Oh to shake out the life we lose in dreams and all those proxy moments beyond our discretion where the will is lost and all the sirens we failed to wake disappear into the void yet those we do remember have never occurred or we could not avoid. When the wind stops and you look out at the silver birch that enjoy only the wet ground around the river then you wonder why you came back to find that beyond all the years there is nothing left but the image of a girl as she walked beside the water. Her white dress contained her virtue at least in your eyes but later you were to find that there was no end to it and you wonder why it mattered so much then. As you looked at her you knew there would be no other ever in your stars. She searched your face as you washed your feet in the water letting loose her red hair and waiting for you to make a move in any direction. You crossed the shallows that seemed so deep but for once you were brave for you knew your life depended upon it if you were to leave even the slightest evidence of your existence. And for that we are bound to gather up our courage so that the light of love should touch whichever shadow we are under.

Kerrisdale

THE SAFETY OF THE SHORE

Tambourines and chanting Byzantines;
I heard them sing in the night.
Then I awoke from dreadful dreams
and waited for the morning light
to explain just what it means
when you cannot open the door
or swim to the safety of the shore.

Kerrisdale

THE CRESCENT OF THE MOON

Pink flower in my hand,
please do not close
when I'm so near to Venus.
Let me suddenly understand
that the crescent of the moon
is the sign for me to enter;
a desire for the center;
and the call of the womb.

Kerrisdale

WHO CAN BE CERTAIN

Sad as a flower that
hides from the rain,
I watch the leaves
harvest in sheaves.
For who can be certain
they will ever fall again.

Kerrisdale

ALL THE JUICES OF BABYLON

You have all the juices of Babylon
so full of the beauty of the world.
Stocked with every female pleasure
yet every charm held in reserve;
of course, being quite aware of them;
such grace is your special preserve.

Kerrisdale

MY TRUE LOVE'S GLISTENING FACE

Oh find me a diamond wheel
that will cut the bright facets
to show and shine as mine,
the glorious glow on my true
loves glistening face.
Oh give me the chance to seal
within her those sweet sachets
and bouquets born of her wine.
Let the first fire of her virgin brew
whirl and whet my loving taste.
In the first flashes of the night
let me find where her rubies hide.
Should I see her lashes slip aside,
I'll know my love is deep inside.

Kerrisdale

SEDUCTION

Ladies who hide behind dark glasses
are taking a chance with romance.
With so many other points to look at
the eyes might decide if they dance.
Ladies...whatever quickens the heart,
is also sure to slow the mind.

Skagen, Denmark

THE NIGHTINGALE

What are the sounds of evening
that only the nightingale shows
an hour before the sun sets and
connects to the brilliance as it goes?
Then all the world listens in
afraid of missing out tonight
on what this singer knows
about that last gasp of light.

Kerrisdale

FATE

Whatever holds the heart
together sometimes fails.
Yet, how are we to know?
For time never warns us
that life is a ship that sails
without lights into the dark.
So flight your feet if you can
far away from the medicine man.
Don't go to the tower on the hill
that soon will have no bell to ring.
Hear your own voice and sing;
douse the lights in your tent;
take a look at the firmament
and try to challenge the stars.

Skagen, Denmark

IT'S NOT OUR DREAMS THAT BIND US

It's not our dreams that bind us
but what is left to remind us
that all the world is ethereal,
sometimes just a conversation
where we speak for everyone;
fill every part in the cast;
every idea is ours; every kiss
is from the heart.
Your words were few
but I heard them all.
I saw you were fair
and walked on air.
As you pass me by
you may hear me sigh...
Hold on to my hand
and try to understand,
it's not our dreams
that bind us together
but what is left behind
to remind us.

Skagen, Denmark

IF THE SUN PICKS OUT A CLOUD

Within all the happy songs,
often there are sad notes
in the air.
Sometimes there's a pause to joy
waiting on the edge of every one
in our care.
If the sun picks out a cloud
for you to hide behind
don't turn your eyes away.
Sadness always leaves the mind
unless you decide it should stay.

Skagen, Denmark

SOUP, BREAD AND JASMINE

Why do hardy hands that hold,
fold, let concern to easily slip away
despite seemingly breakneck love?
There's soup and bread and jasmine
mixed with the usual eager event.
Not really love just endearment
amidst the long planned journeys.
Then…the sadness of a shipwreck.
Loneliness returns to the world;
can't find a place worth hiding in;
somersaults mindlessly, at random.

Skagen, Denmark

47

FRANKINCENSE

There was a faint whiff of frankincense
and it took me to your tented oasis. Within,
the perfume pierced your desert secrets
and drew my lips to your silken skin.
Yet, was this just an amorous dream?
Or is desire the cold misted morning
when little birds look for cream
and love strikes without warning?
Oh, if love has made any sense
then off and away with pretense!
'Tis better to die in the seeking,
than to suffer without its keeping.

Skagen, Denmark

ALL WILL STILL BE WELL

What moments, hours, days
have passed over thee
as you waited for me.
When the bell was rung
a song of all your ways
a poem of every rhyme
the art of your design
broke open my tender shell.
Should everything else be lost
but you, all will still be well.

Skagen, Denmark

DON'T GET TOO EXCITED

When summer is but a flight of fiction
and a lovely woman looks at you.
It's what she feels that matters
and not your expectations.

Skagen, Denmark

WHO WILL LET US KNOW?

How many horizons
do we have to cross
to exhaust what we owe?
If one lifetime is not enough
then who will let us know?

Skagen, Denmark

SONG OF AN OLD ARAB TO THE JEWS IN 1948

I look out into the distance
across the wasteland
these upstarts dream about.
My eyes grow tired
at the lack of colour.
Save for the fig trees
there is little that blooms;
I am even forbidden the wine
that consoles other men.
If there was a cool mound
I would climb it to the top;
but this dry sterile country
has no snow on the hills.
All of the rivers lie
like its soul, salted, sunken.
The life is sluggish as a donkey
or angry like a parched camel
baring its yellow teeth.
Jewish fellow, what do you covet
that we have foregone so long?
From what fertile ground
will your green dreams come?
You could not come for comfort.

Show us where the treasures are
that we may fathom the faith
feeding the long travail to get here
and can lend you less bitterness.

Cloverdale

THE MORE I HAVE TO HIDE

Horses cough among chestnuts
while the wind blows away
the wavering yellow sunset.
Emotions come out of me
that only a woman can bring.
She was early and beautiful,
at least to my eager eyes.
And I was only as honorable
as she desired me to be.
The piece she took away
with her left an open wound.
So at the end of the day
the more I have to say
to contain all my pride,
the more I have to hide.

Kerrisdale

WE'VE BEEN EVERYWHERE BEFORE

Oh how white the whimsy
that has a hold on us;
treads in our footsteps;
yet does not follow
in those courtly dances
as we follow our heart
and only kiss tender hands
that are proffered up to us.
But we have been there before.
We've been everywhere before.

Kerrisdale

A STREET CORNER POET DURING A MINER'S STRIKE

Is your conscience
still in your pockets?
If it comes back
to your spotted hearts
remember.......
these are its messengers.
Look you upon them!
If there's a God
these are his lilies.
If there's a heaven
here are his angels;
no other hell for them.
Don't sit too close
to your firesides,
there's blood in the heat.

London

PUT YOUR LOVE BESIDE THE FLOWERS

Beauty can be put away
but not forgotten.
Its light will always shine.
Put your love
beside the flowers,
and let it grow with them.

Kerrisdale

EVERY WOMAN MAY HAVE A SECRET HEART

For who knows
what a woman
overcomes for
the love of a man.
Every woman may
have a secret heart
hidden away
from the world.
Her light
is what we know.
Her shade is the mystery.

Kerrisdale

WHERE ARE THE LOVE SONGS

Where are the love songs
we could not start,
the stories not written?
Where the uncertain art
and my music whose sound
I have lost and cannot play?
Whatever comes
will be out of me;
whatever its guise
it will not matter.
It may come too soon
or perhaps too late.
Would we wish it
otherwise?
Love too is, as always,
the surprise of fate.

Kerrisdale

YOU WILL HURRY ON

You must not regret
the wind the sun
or the rain;
for you will hurry on.
You must not forget
the joy the love
or the pain;
for you will hurry on.
When your faith falters
you must renew
the buttress;
because some candles
are never lit and some
never go out;
but you will hurry on.
A sailor who must catch
the southwest wind
and is never sure
when there will be
another;
he too will hurry on.
Those who let love
leak out secretly
like radiation,
and by proxy;
living like oxy-morons
should take it, take it,
never break it break it.

They will be faithful
when they hurry on.
The maker
might have a catalogue,
perhaps an index
or a bibliography,
but you must write
the chapter pages
before you hurry on.

Kerrisdale

A CONVERSATION

The young woman sat alone,
counting a string of white pearls
round her fingers like a rosary.
"Look at that woman there!
She is not very beautiful,
why do you like her so much?"
"I imagine she has a garden
and can't wait for the Spring."

Skagen, Denmark.

YOUR MUSIC WAS WRONG

Octagonal tiles upon the floor
a fancy knocker on the door.
Oh, come in and be happy.
Oh, come in and be happy.
I listened to your exquisite quotes
striking, like notes on a grand piano;
romance as always my favorite flavor;
you, the player had me sing your song.
I really loved the lyrics,
alas, your music was wrong.

Skagen, Denmark.

LOVE LOOKING OUT OF YOUR EYES

While the church candles
burn to yellow and I see
my lonely cherry tree
fading from pearl to white;
all the diffident daffodils
are hanging their heads
as we are saying good night.
I kiss your cherubic hands
clasped like the Mona Lisa.
Love looking out of your eyes
has taken me by surprise.

Kerrisdale

THE SMILE OF A WOMAN

Whatever is beautiful
does not fall into place
so easily.
And yet it cannot
be put there
without care.
Here is the light
there the shade;
here is a bridge
to be crossed.
To live, a fish
must jump.
When everything is known
yet nothing so simple
can fall into place
so easily.
The stimulus the rise and fall
of a woman's breast
is invisible.
Like the wind in the sails
the shadows of the clouds,
all beauty accumulates above.
Finally, the greatest mystery;
the smile of a woman in love.

Kerrisdale

A FATHER'S LETTER TO A SON IN THE TRENCHES

You've been away too long
and I miss you.
Positioned I am in a special place,
bidden into it by the welcome
in the early morning, remember,
by the trace of a single bird
melody meandering up the line
from creature to creature, far enough
to complete the circle; keeping
their crisp sense of the earth.
I shall set off down the hill
where the roads crossing over
bodes the farmer to open white
five bar gates towards the mill.
I know this fellow has a desire
for energy that swells the grape;
for wind that shivers the almond.
His grain never bursts to yellow.
In the distance the long carse
with a middle space for a gate
and a single cypress that draws
a stark landscape for the stars.
Up the old clay road I can go,
remain, to look at it descend,
watch it bend towards the plain,
that valley green lying below.
It's not too far for us to call
to the old battered farmhouse

worn away washing tubs hanging
protecting perhaps its ancient wall.
There in wicker chairs set at noon
I spy the dame and her daughter
who sit and smell the perfume of lupin
in the soft shades of juicy July.
But soon the man they have on hire,
his stooks at the gable, looks at the sun
for the sign that he and the dog
bring back the kine to the byre.
You can hear them between the birches;
smell the baggage in his one horse cart
as he brings home cows and turnips
and sometimes fresh cut cabbage.
Come on let's go! Up past the quarry
that built every cottage around
in the hushed not so long ago.
Stroll past the century old church
where men who worked with stone
were never content with a wall
or a parapet or fancy ramps.
They must exercise the artisan
must make the lifeblood known,
freeze the spirit with banisters
balustrades and columns. Stamps,
that only an artist can seize.
And then..........
listen with me while the old priest speaks:

*While I live the life divine they feed me with bread and cheese and I can
still sup
from the cup they fill with their wine;*

looking at every star when I have the time.
The new bride's perfume
can't distract my eye
as she passes me by,
her soft voice whispering
as green feral corn through a fence
can seduce the animal in all of us.
I possess a virgin world each night
and she's not a maid by morn.'

Thus did I survive when I was down the pit
and became fused to death every day.
The dreams of our fathers have come and gone
and I still have no cup to dip my roses in
or catch the place upon the earth
where a quiet mind has noble reflections
of all that went before, all that is to come.
Goodnight my son, I'll go back to my dreams,
and see if you have joined me."
You've been away too long,
and I miss you.

Skagen, Denmark

MAY 15TH, 1948

Yesterday, in the late spring,
the State of Israel was declared,
yet these are winter days
with sadness wrapped up in them.
There are no marching bands here,
no drummers, no frogs singing in the night.
The people we saw in the stripes
behind the wire in '44 and '45,
who tarnished our souls
with the final horror
of the darkness suffered,
have arrived on the shore
of the promised land
promised once more.
They escaped the yaw of Europe;
held offshore they stink in leaky boats;
Now they die by the hundreds. And we
liberators, allow them cloth of many colours,
yet put them back behind the wire.
On this beach where they stand
like animals holding out their children
for food to soldiers who cried
the last time they saw them in chains,
now move them from one zoo to another.
Look how alien they are yet familiar.
It is forbidden to throw them bread.
The same faces stare out
this time their children are with them,

they are seeing us with bitter eyes.
The unmerciful past has set in
they mean to have us join their suffering.
Behind this shore in the hinterland
there lie in wait another clan.
In these hills there is no gold
a bitter salt is close to the surface.
It has no promise no milk, no honey.
It seems even its poverty is seen
as sweet between their feet.
Yet men will not share the sand
where God's goodness no longer exists,
points out the barrenness of our future.

Falcon Cove, Oregon

GRETCHEN OPENED THE SHUTTERS

Gretchen opened the shutters
and the light washed in so softly
she had no need to shade her eyes
at the inroad.
The little table by the window
held a plate of yellow persimmons
reflecting the light
against the wall, in gold.
An open book of Gongora's poetry
lay in the shadows.
The branch of an orange tree
caught by the slats was unfastened.
Tenderly, she held it to her face,
rewarded by the redolence
that took away the early morning
mustiness of the room
still full of their slumbers, and love.
Her drowsy eyes were laden
with the madness of the south;
her ears stuffed with the slight
movement of air
that touched the leaves
making them restless.
Stretching her body awake,
becoming aware
her lover was admiring her.
She did not turn fully to him,
only moving her body in slow

dipping curves;
moaning a little at the effort.
Stopping for a moment
placing her hands in the water jug,
then, with a moist movement
touching her breasts
and cheeks; gathering
her loose hair; tying
it behind her head
to reveal more
of the ivory neck.
Only then did she turn
and let the full light fall
on her liquid body.
Hands above her head
returning to his arms
still warm, still full of love,
still needed, still welcome.
As they embraced
the swallows
screeched outside.
A church bell reminded them
of candles
lit the night before;
red for wishes and dreams
against the uncertainties
of love.
As the friar took the tariff
he smiled,
his black eyes flickering
for a moment
in the candlelight.

He had a part of their dream
and his aged face softened,
he nodded his head
in a subtle movement
that found them holding
hands tightly for a moment.
Then, it seemed necessary
to bend a little
with the soul.
For some reason
some essence
of their desire
for each other
leaked out to the priest.
It wasn't begrudged,
and he knew it.

Barcelona Spain

I HARDLY KNOW A WORD YOU SAY TO ME

Woman with the soft heart,
I hardly know a word
you say to me.
We speak a different
language, you see.
Yet when we say
that we're in love
then all our words
seem to sound the same.
I only hope that I
can keep your heart.
But most of all that
we can keep this love.
That part of us
that feels the same,
though I hardly know
a word you say to me.

Kerrisdale

HERE, IN APRIL

As I savor oranges from Sevilla,
the leaves here just creep out
quietly in April.
Later, I will reach again to favor
the black olives from Andalucia.
Perhaps then a peach, always the best
I can get from farther to the west.
I imagine Catalan cherry blossoms
pink and white and merry in the wind.
But our young boys know it's too early
yet to ask what buttercups under
a young girl's chin will say.
For here in April the world
is not green or golden
or hot until May.

Kerrisdale

OF MORE TENDER TIMES

A world covered in corn;
the midsummer leaves
yellow and green,
yet warm. In the sedge
May flowers still fresh
and full of colour
growing on the edge
of the wold worn world.
And in every valley
between the seasons
softly spoken rhymes
of more tender times.
Nothing more to need
nothing more to heed.

Skagen, Denmark.

HOW ELSE COULD WE EXPLAIN

Ill timed is the lack
of appetite for love.
Is to miss the spice
that makes of life
a match for rest.
To have left no space
for all that worthy is,
we may be set to miss
whatever then is blest.
Wherever there is darkness
there also may be light;
perhaps 'tis trite to say so.
But on unknown paths forward
can our respite afford to go;
though the large and little
that we have come to know
may later turn, be brittle.
Then, if bright be our sight
that can burn a starless night,
so, when there was no sun
no, nor moon, nor blessing,
how else could we explain
that we had not lived again?

Kerrisdale

THERE WILL ALWAYS BE SOMEONE TO LOVE

There will always be
someone to love.
One with a kind heart
and a gentle hand.
Even if it's the only
faith you have,
then believe......
there will always be
someone to love.

Kerrisdale

WHO CHOOSES?

Who chooses
the lilacs we place
in our crystal vases?
Opens all the doors
for early flowers
and welcomes them home
from the colder shores.
Who chooses
the dreams of the night
we forget in the light?
Who chooses
the heart we love so much
yet are not able to touch?
Who turns our face
to the stars in the sky
but lets the morning Venus
set, then pass us by?
Of course we'll never know.
But that doesn't soften
the blow.

Kerrisdale

I PLEAD GUILTY, M'LUD

Wrestling in the mud!
That is no place for love.
It can't continue
in a feather bed
when the bird has flown.
It has to stop
when temperatures drop.
If only we had known
and not lost our head.
No point sending flowers
of passion in the last hours.
But then, those tender arms around
your neck. What the heck!
I plead guilty M'lud.

Kerrisdale

FLOWERS NOT SMILING NOW

No matter; I looked.

Love wasn't there;
nothing to share.

It's solitude for me.

The corner of my eye,
over my left shoulder
it seems, has dreams.

They will be, I suppose,
reduced to poetry; might
be just a page of prose.

The last line of sight
was in the gardens at Kew.

Flowers not smiling now;
not without you.

Kerrisdale

I WON'T BE KISSED TODAY

From out of the night
all my cozened charms
came away, burning bright.
But my lover took too long
to bring and sing her song.
The wind flew southwest
just like Shelley, P.B.
said it would be;
it blew her heat away;
I won't be kissed today.
A winter's tale she made of it
of the time and the dreams
it takes when the heart awakes
and all those gifts parade
with promises new love makes;
I won't be kissed today.
Whatever plans we lovers had
whatever plays were laid,
now look less good than bad.
I know the price I paid;
I won't be kissed today.

Kerrisdale

ALL I KNOW, IS YOUR NAME

Oh soft loveliness speak.
Let me hear your voice.
All I know is your name.
I admire you from afar.
Yet I've imagined
that perhaps in time
in my dreams once
I kissed your breast
as if it might carry
your blood into mine.
Was that soundless spell
just an idol's idle token?
If all I ever know
is your name
I will die quietly,
and free of fame.
If I should lack
forever, a word,
a chord of love
a tithe from thee,
must the flowers die
the birds be muffled,
the winds turn to fly
neither north or south
nor to east or the west?

Oh soft loveliness speak.
Let me hear your voice.
All I know, is your name.

Kerrisdale

WELCOME MONDAY MORNING

Welcome Monday morning!
But where is the moon?
Is it hiding with Venus
and crying out loud
behind our carbon cloud?
Missing the Earth rising
once so blue and white.
Now, like all the rest,
just reflected light.

Kerrisdale

LOOKING FOR LOVE AND DREAMING

What dreams I've had!
What moments seized
without my knowledge,
and selectively minded.
A world of fertile shadows
haphazardly, hardily shaped.
Of rivers over waterfalls
perishing on rocks below,
yet extending the stream
into a trombone tender sloe.
Lovers from behind a sheet;
often met on an empty street;
and lips that tasted so sweet.
Where white birds take off
from a limpid lake steaming,
and me with nothing
but a set of poems
in my pocket, looking
for love, and dreaming.

Kerrisdale

AS LOVE LOST BY THE WILL

There are places
we may not enter
and had better shun
than ever look upon
what has not been granted.
Nor all the letters sent
yet never opened
closed like the heart
that was shattered
and cannot fall whole
from heaven again
unless by faith
if you believe in it.
Nothing passes so ill
as love lost by the will.

Kerrisdale

GOD'S GRACE BE WITH YOU

There is no doubt
it once fell on me.
Though I could not see
the warm woman's body
that was my comfort;
God's grace be upon her;
to the woman he sent
to pass her lips
over my eyes.
Twice, I've had his grace,
now I beg for yours,
a smile upon your face.
God did not take away
all my senses,
only the judgement,
the choice of my eyes;
he let me hear a woman's
voice, and then her sighs.

Kerrisdale

NO SECOND COMING

Salute the seasons!
Praise the Earth!
There are no leaves
falling on the moon.
No rain cleansing Mars.
Whatever time shatters
might not fall whole
from Heaven again,
unless by faith:
if you believe in it.

Kerrisdale

SUNDAY MORNING

What can be more spiritual
than the deflection of misfortune
the jettison of worldly goods
for the uncertainty of faith
and the quietness of the inner voice
one hears above all others?

Kerrisdale

SUPERSTITION

My mother said to open
doors and windows
to summon cool air
she knew wasn't there.
She was superstitious,
it was the shadows
she feared, not the heat.
There were times
when her magnolia
lost attraction;
though still in possession
of its scents.
Wisdom comes late.
Weather, vain in the head
points in all directions.
We go our own way,
instead.

Kerrisdale

WHAT LOVE CAN TELL ME

Heaven knows
or does it?
How the world
has turned upon me
to split my spirit
between one God
and another.
And now, my lover
beckons me
to choose
another way
to heaven,
with what love
can tell me.

Kerrisdale

ACTOR TURNS TO THE AUDIENCE..........

If I should see her again
what could I say
that would persuade her
to consider me
above all others?
Is she out of my reach?
Look! I watch her walk
among her admirers
flashing her eyes
to all comers, yet
never at me.
What could I say
that would attract her?

Kerrisdale

YOU MUST NOT LOOK AT ME WITH EYES LIKE THAT

You must not look at me
with eyes like that;
as if a pavilion of lights
had suddenly been sighted.
If you should skate away
the ice will never hold
the weight, of my sadness.
Who knows any of the beginning
or especially, the ending of this?
But what will it matter my lady,
so long as your hair is still red
there is no ring on your finger
and you and I leave everything
unsaid.

Kerrisdale

TROUBADOURS BEGIN THEIR SONGS

"Oh such fine women we have
They feel like silk
smell like jasmine
skin cool as white wine

Alas, our hearts are in famine
From lack of their substance
So only by our song
Can we find where we belong.

How slowly does the earth turn
While we wait for the spring
To course and flood and burn
Through flesh we dare not touch.

The place of whatsoever
we did not say
will never come back,
unless perhaps in verse.
Yet what could be worse
than to recognize our errors,
heart breaks, disappointments,
disguised as art?

Kerrisdale

HAND ME DOWN TO THE DEVIL

Hand me down to the devil
if I've hurt your heart
too hastily.
I know that your sweetness
can take the curdle
from my blood,
and manage my moods
with a tender hand,
or a turn of the head
away, from what I've said.
If I was off to the crusades,
or to any farther shore
I would miss you more
than a poem can say,
or to wait another day
for you to walk my way.

Kerrisdale

A WOMAN IN LOVE

A change in the wind,
perhaps an omen
hardly noticed, saying;
Don't look for diamonds
in the sky, or true love
that will never die.
All hearts are softly born.
This girl may start unworldly,
yet harden as time goes on.
A hazard in the wind,
perhaps an omen to go by:
when tears drop from her eye.
She looks so happy now,
such a smile upon her face.
Nothing in the world
to trouble her,
and a man full of love
to embrace

Kerrisdale

CHOICES

Of all the choices ever made,
some are just a mockery
in light and shade.
Others, perhaps the crockery
our mother mislaid.
As the eye of lust rejoices
there are other voices
heard only by the brave.
Decisions are for a Quean,
or her man, to choose between.
None......are for a knave

Kerrisdale

WHY SHOULD WE LET OTHERS DREAM FOR US?

If time is your only impediment
remove the clocks and calendars
the diaries and the memorabilia
photographs and lucky charms.
Turn out the music and books,
the dark lady, the handsome man.
Embrace the mountain chickadee
and the sun rising and setting,
search for Venus in the morning.
"Within your mind is the world."
At least that's what Buddha said.
Other people are also full of advice
as if they were better examples.
Perhaps to consider: Just a thought.
Why should we let others dream for us?

Kerrisdale

WE CANNOT CHOOSE OUR ISLAND

We cannot choose our island.
Though it may be the territory
of the failed harvest
and the unknown sickness.
We made a sacrifice;
why didn't it work?
The sky is still dry,
the air full of dust,
the children may die,
mothers have to say goodbye,
fathers lose their trust.
Yet, some despise the nay sayers
with no faith in their prayers.
We cannot choose our island.

Kerrisdale

TRUEST ALWAYS, AT FIRST SIGHT

The spirits that move us
surge up in the blood
and can't be held down
or as much understood
as the end of childhood,
when all dreams begin.
Then our needs are known
and are so hard to avoid.
Though slipping to fantasy,
consumate, in the real world.
Earth below, heaven above,
and always a place for love;
just like Venus in the light,
truest always, at first sight.

Kerrisdale

A MOORISH POET IN ANDALUCIA

I wondered early
if this was a good place
for happiness.
Everything is so strange.
The faces; the way
that water runs down
so fast from green hills
to the sea.
We came with drawn swords
in hand to conquer this land,
and in the end it overcame us.
I love the winter feel of it
in the mountains.
I've come a long way
to find such coolness,
yet, with the occasional
warm wind to remind me
of the desert.
I've set off a crowd
of cherry trees
in my new garden,
whilst lying at ease
eating figs, writing poems
that may travel east,
so that my brothers

might know that love
exists everywhere;
and that my sisters
will smile and say:
"The woman hasn't
changed him."

Kerrisdale

THE SPRING DOTH COME UPON US

If on stones now the blossoms fall,
nature still will leap the wall.
The Spring doth come upon us,
and whatever Nature grows,
grows within us all at once.
Though its flowers
cannot feed the flesh
they do affect the blood,
bringing it to a head;
cosseting the heart;
venturing the voice; thus,
the Spring doth come upon us.

Kerrisdale

PAMPER ME WITH SCARLET POPPIES

Pamper me with scarlet poppies,
hug me among pink and red hyacinths;
then you can touch my breast,
and my lips, with all the rest.
Yes, say I'm elegant and sweet,
like the apple tinted rose
you may still place at my feet.

Kerrisdale

JUST A TASTE OF THE WORLD

It was just a taste of the world
held in the mouth, felt in the heart,
where all despair.
Dreams don't fall from heaven
yet they may take us there.
If ever there was a woman
so closely cosseted in white
and walking so carefully
among carmen colored tables
and who by the twist
of her little louis heeled foot....

Oh woe is me!
What will she do with me?
Such dreams do not fall from heaven
yet may surely take us there.

YOUR FACE

Barely has night fallen,

when my first thought

in the silent darkness is,

to dream about you;

recompense for the clamor

of a joyless, absent day.

And in that stripped void

when time was nonsense,

I eked out an effortless passion

where my love was given sway.

Thus, my dream is a likely place,

no matter where my pillow,

to find your face.

STILL TELL ME THAT YOU LOVE ME

Please tell me that you love me,

even if your voice whispers it

so softly as the grasshopper lark;

still tell me that you love me.

More renown I cannot know

than the lisp from your lips,

a covert love, from one so fair.

As you came within my reach

close, like *Venus looking at the moon*,

your perfume overran my room;

still, I needed to know you loved me.

Kerrisdale

THE STARS LINE UP

The stars line up and

show me the way to go.

They shine on whatever

I did not know.

Is there more in Heaven

than our eyes can show?

I am not so foolish that

I cannot find a dream

with the tides of the moon,

the lapping of the sea,

and you.

Kerrisdale

THE FIRST DAYS OF JUNE

What does love say

in the face of loss?

If my love is true

what more could be said

to you?

Whatever settles into

the heart, can never

break apart.

We didn't reach the moon,

but this is December.

I am trying to remember

the first days of June.